Beverly A Nance

Take Care

Copyright © 2018 by Beverly A. Nance

All rights reserved. This book or any portion thereof may not be reproduced or used in any manner whatsoever without the express written permission of the publisher except for the use of brief quotations in a book review.

Printed in the United States of America

This book is not intended as a substitute for the medical advice of physicians. The reader should regularly consult a physician on matters relating to his/her health and particularly with respect to any symptoms that may require diagnosis or medical attention

To Troy and Tylar Jenkins,

my WHY for everything I do.

Table of Contents

Take Care i

My Take iii

What to Expect from This Book vii

Chapter 1 School Days 1

Chapter 2 Married with Children 3

Chapter 3 Reactions from the World 7

Chapter 4 DIVORCE 9

Chapter 5 RELOCATION 11

Chapter 6 WHAT DOES CAREGIVING REALLY MEAN?
.... 15

Chapter 7 CAREGIVING AND PARENTING 16

Chapter 8 CAREGIVER STRESS 18

Chapter 9 FINANCIAL STRESS 23

Chapter 10 TAKE CARE OR BURN OUT 31

Chapter 11 TAKE CARE OR DEPRESSION 38

Chapter 12 TAKE CARE TO EAT BETTER 42

Chapter 13 TAKE CARE BY EXERCISING MORE 46

Chapter 14 TAKE CARE SLEEP MORE 49

Chapter 15 TAKE CARE OF THE F-WORD: FRUSTRATION 51

Chapter 16 ISOLATION 54

Chapter 17 TAKE CARE OF GUILT 56

Chapter 18 Set Boundaries, Say No 60

Chapter 19 FIND A HOBBY 63

Chapter 20 LAUGH A LOT 65

Chapter 21 TAKE CARE OF YOUR SPIRITUALITY 66

Chapter 22 GRATITUDE 69

Chapter 23 Volunteering 70

Chapter 24 PAPERWORK 72

Chapter 25 9 to 5 73

Chapter 26 IS IT TOO MUCH? 77

Chapter 27 THINK POSITIVE, KEEP HOPE ALIVE 81

Chapter 28 EXPRESS YOURSELF 85

Chapter 29 GOLDEN YEARS 87

Chapter 30 YOU ARE NOT ALONE 89

Chapter 31 RESENTMENT 91

Chapter 32 MI CASA SU CASA 94

Chapter 33 I'M THE BOSS, NO I'M THE BOSS 96

Chapter 34 COIN CONTRIBUTION 98

Chapter 35 THIS NOT THAT 100

Chapter 36 HAVE A PLAN B 102

Chapter 37 KEEP DREAMING 104

Chapter 38 REWARDS 107

Chapter 39 TAKE CARE, YOU MATTER 109

Chapter 40 TAKE CARE TIMESAVERS FOR CAREGIVERS 111

Take Care

"There are only four kinds of people in the world - those who have been caregivers, those who are caregivers, those who will be caregivers and those who will need caregivers."

— *Rosalyn Carter*

My Take

If you are a woman or a man who has been searching for a comprehensive resource that explains how to survive and keep your sanity while being a caregiver for a loved one or how to be a successful caregiving employee in a straightforward way, then this book is for you! But before we get to all of that, let me tell you a bit more about who I am and what I hope to share with you.

My name is Beverly Nance. Some of you may already be familiar with my brand, Puzzlebilities®. I am a business owner, best-selling author, civic leader, storyteller, and, more importantly, I am a mother and caregiver. I have written for *Autism Parenting* magazine and been featured in *The Story Exchange*, as well as local publications and blogs. I frequently get questions like, *"Is it hard raising an autistic daughter?"* or *"How do you work full-time and be a caregiver?"* or *"How do you balance caregiving and staying sane?"*

After getting so many inquiries about caregiving and autism, and realizing I had so much information to share, it just made perfect sense to write a book about caregiving life. Yes, I am a mother and caregiver of a daughter who has autism, but I want to emphasize that I'm also just a woman who wants to feel good, laugh and enjoy life.

Taking care of myself is a significant part of that. While writing this book, I frequently referred back to all the knowledge I've acquired through the years about caregiving and autism. As you might imagine, I have spent countless hours with other parents and professionals in the caregiving space, so this book will be part introspective, part educational, and even a bit humorous at times.

I thought long and hard about what I wanted to include in this book, and when I first conceptualized it, I knew that I wanted to get personal about my own caregiving experience and my perspective on caregiving life.

I should start by saying that I am a woman who did not know anything about autism when my daughter was born. For the first couple of years after she was diagnosed with autism, I was in learning mode but secretly in denial. I wanted to find a cure rather than deal with the symptoms. But as you can see, I never managed to achieve finding that cure and I jumped into advocate mode pretty quickly.

So much of who we are and how we perceive ourselves is intricately tied to our children. This book is about caregiving life but is also about a deeper message, one of self-care and knowing that life is good and full of possibilities. There is a great interconnectedness between how caregivers feel about those they care for and how caregivers feel about taking care of themselves. In many ways, caregivers take better care of those they care for and let their own care fall by the wayside.

Thank you so much for taking the time to read my book. I hope you find the information in it to be extremely helpful as you go through your caregiving day. It is always a good feeling when someone hears your caregiving story and tells you to "take care" of yourself and "hang in there." But it is even a better feeling when YOU can say the same to yourself.

What to Expect from This Book

This book is about life as a caregiver. Some of us become caregivers for life and others become caregivers for short periods of time. Whether you are in it for the short term or the long haul the premise is the same. Caregiving is not easy, and it can take a toll on your life.

In the beginning, I'll share my caregiving story and, I'll be blunt, I've had a pretty rocky time as a caregiver. Nevertheless, I want to share my caregiving struggles and lessons with you. Many of us have plenty of stories to tell when it comes to taking care of others or being taken care of. Ultimately, the purpose of sharing my caregiving story is to show you where I came from and where I am now.

After my story, I will get into the good, bad, ugly, and rewards of being a caregiver. We'll cover topics like patience, stress, family, and resources, to name a few. We will also cover how to deal with professionals to secure help and how to gain and maintain life balance, as well as how to deal with emergencies.

I wanted to make this book a go-to source for all things caregiving so if you see caregiving as a part of your present or future, this book is definitely for you.

Chapter 1
School Days

When I was a kid my dream was to become a teacher. I attended Valencia Park Elementary school in San Diego, California. My 3rd-grade teacher was named Ms. Howard. I was in awe of her and I wanted to be just like her. I clung to her every word and I thought to be a teacher was the best career choice for me. By the time I reached high school my love of the classroom had not changed, only now I was clinging to every word of my English teacher, Ms. Gabay. I loved reading and writing and thought perhaps I would become a high school English teacher just like her. Upon high school graduation, my worldview changed my dreams of becoming a teacher. By the time I graduated and was accepted to San Diego State University I no longer wanted to teach; the only problem now was that I didn't know exactly what I wanted to do but I had an acceptance letter and my parents were willing to pay for my education, so I enrolled in undergrad classes and fell in love with learning several subjects. By my third year in college, I still didn't know which career direction I wanted to take but I was now majoring in Public Administration. My dad and sister were working for the United States

Postal Service and my dad suggested I take the test when it opened. I took the test and thanks to my sister Diane, I aced it, was hired, and now I was earning my own money, working nights and attending school during the day. When my grades began to suffer, and I struggled to stay awake at work, I made the fateful decision to drop out of school, promising myself I would return later and finish my degree. Working for the Postal Service was interesting. The process of a letter being mailed and reaching mailboxes worldwide is underrated. Postal workers process mail twenty-four hours a day and deliver six, sometimes seven, days per week. They work crazy hours and holidays to ensure businesses receive communications, kids receive birthday presents from far and wide, customers receive advertisements, and Grandma gets a nice card from her grandkids. The work that postal workers do is crucial and much needed, and I hope they will continue to find ways to evolve in this world of e-everything.

Chapter 2
Married with Children

I met my ex-husband at work. He was a mailhandler and I was a clerk. We dated for a few years before we got married. We married, had a son (Troy), purchased a house on a quiet cul-de-sac, had a daughter (Tylar), and were living the American dream. My son and my daughter were both born prematurely, my daughter by Cesarean at 4 pounds 1 ounce. I made the decision to have a tubal ligation while I was having my Cesarean. When I was younger I always said I wanted to have five children, but after having two children born pre-maturely I abandoned that idea. If you have ever given birth to a child and had to leave them in the Intensive Care Unit while you are discharged from the hospital, then you know what a gut-wrenching feeling that can be. Fortunately, Tylar did not have to stay in the hospital for long and was at home where she belonged. She was so tiny and cute. I had a son and a daughter, and I felt on top of the world. Tylar was typically developing but did not show any interest in talking, and when I looked a little harder I noticed she would not give eye contact or show an interest in interacting with others. Well-meaning family members told me not to worry, but it was worrying me. I watched my son meet his milestones, walking, taking, pretend play, holding a spoon. My daughter, except for walking, wasn't doing any of these things. I took her to the doctor and held my breath, not wanting to hear that there was anything wrong with my baby girl. She was first diagnosed with pervasive developmental disorder. I had never heard of it, so I rushed home to research what exactly held her hostage. In my research, all I saw was the word "autism" and it was rightly so because I pressed for a true diagnosis and was told that she had autism. When a parent learns that there is a problem with their child's development, this information comes as a tremendous blow. Hearing that my daughter had autism was heartbreaking. If you know anything about autism, you know that there is no cure, no definitive cause. Autism, or autism spectrum disorder, refers to a range of conditions characterized by challenges with social skills, repetitive behaviors, speech and nonverbal communication, as well as by unique strengths and differences. While those with autism may display similar characteristics, everyone with autism is different.

The term "spectrum" reflects the wide variation in challenges and strengths possessed by each person with autism.

Autism's most-obvious signs tend to appear between 2 and 3 years of age. In some cases, it can be diagnosed as early as 18 months. Some developmental delays associated with autism can be identified and addressed even earlier. It is estimated that 1 in 59 children in the United States is autistic, and this includes 1 in 42 boys and 1 in 189 girls. An estimated 50,000 teens with autism become adults – and lose school-based autism services – each year. Around one-third of people with autism remain nonverbal. Tylar has very little language, most of which is echolalia (repeating back what is said). Around one-third of people with autism have an intellectual disability. Certain medical and mental health issues frequently accompany autism. They include gastrointestinal (GI) disorders, seizures, sleep disturbances, attention deficit and hyperactivity disorder (ADHD), anxiety, and phobias. Tylar has sleep disturbances, seizures, and anxiety.

The public Beverly thought Tylar would learn to talk, she would have friends, and she would grow up normal with a lot of help from doctors and therapists. The private Beverly was devastated. I cried in the shower so my kids would not hear me. I questioned God. I went through denial, grief, fear, anger, guilt, confusion, powerlessness, disappointment, and rejection. The diagnosis of autism was truly a gut-punch. I wanted to know why her, why us, why me? I searched the internet and read autism forums. I did a ton of research. I found out that I was not alone. I reached out to other parents who have autistic children and that began my journey.

My first and still-best resource was an organization named CARD. CARD stands for the Center for Autism and Related Disorders. My second-best resource was a married couple from Los Angeles who were lawyers and who were the parents of autistic twins. The wife became my daughter's lawyer and together they helped me fight the San Diego Unified School District and receive CARD services. My third-best resource was the Regional Center. My daughter received years of services which helped her learn to say some words, identify numbers and letters, and deal with social situations. Tylar had to learn to use the bathroom, hold utensils, dress, and brush her teeth. While she was able to learn some things, she was still clearly behind.

The thing that bothered me most was her lack of language. She learned to say some words but not clearly. I understood her because I was with her daily. She learned the pecs system and we modified it with items she could relate to, but she always reverted back to pointing or using our hands to signal what she wanted. Her school years were very challenging. Having a lawyer to call was a lifesaver, and having a lawyer who was also a special needs parent was the biggest bonus ever. Every mediation with the school district was settled in my daughter's favor. She was able to benefit from CARD services in our home, as well as having a CARD assistant in school with her. Sadly, parents have to fight for these services. Our school district was out of compliance with the law during this time and a lot of parents had to seek outside services to aid the education of their children. As the years progressed, I came to realize that when you have a special needs child you have to fight and advocate for everything. I became an aggressive advocate for Tylar. Sadly, a lot of parents succumb to the constant fight for services. It's easy to become depressed and worried when you have limited financial resources and limited information.

Chapter 3
Reactions from the World

It's always interesting to witness how friends and family react when I tell them my daughter has autism. There are so many people who were just like me and did not know what autism was, and I have learned to accept that some people do not know, nor do they care. For those that care, I always explain what autism is and how it manifests itself in my daughter. Because autism is a spectrum disorder, there are those that are high functioning, low functioning, and everything in between. Although more and more people are aware of autism, there is still a lot of misinformation. I tend to explain the basics and move on to focus on my daughter's behaviors that they may have noticed. For example, if Tylar has a meltdown while visiting family or friends, it might be because she has a hard time handling changes in her routine, which is common for those with autism. Tylar will give you a kiss on the cheek but does not respond well to being hugged. She uses self-stimulatory behavior such as playing with beads to keep herself calm and feel safe. No, there is not currently a cure and no, I do not know the cause of her autism. Hopefully, those that care will research autism as it pertains to Tylar and the world rather than go with the stereotypical perception (everyone is not "Rain Man").

There have been times in my life that I have witnessed strangers be more sympathetic, curious, and open to learning than family and friends, and that's okay and you need to be okay with that also. Anticipate difficult reactions and embrace those that are willing to understand and be supportive.

Chapter 4
DIVORCE

To say that having a child with a disability takes a toll on a marriage would be unfair to all the married couples who remain committed and in love. I cannot say that the demise of my marriage had anything to do with parenting a child with autism. I know that my filing for divorce from my ex-husband had everything to do with his behavior and my unwillingness to continue in that atmosphere. I wanted better for myself and my son and daughter deserved better.

In California, it's called "irreconcilable differences" and to explain it all would be another book; therefore, I will say I filed for divorce and we began a four-year process of courtrooms, lawyers, child custody agreements, fighting, broken promises, finally ending with me throwing in the towel and relocating to Atlanta, Georgia. I enjoyed living in San Diego, but I no longer felt safe to do so and I wanted to move far away from my ex-husband. I transferred my job and started over in a city that was new to me.

My fresh start in Atlanta immediately got off to a rocky start when I was forced to return to San Diego three times to attend family court. In California, child support is determined by the amount of time you spend with your children. My ex-husband spent years in court attempting to avoid paying child support only to end up paying the maximum when he refused to comply with court orders of supervised visitation. Prior to moving to Atlanta, my ex-husband had not seen our children for nearly a year. He was eventually granted visitation; however, that was ordered to take place over the phone or in Atlanta.

My children have not heard from their father. He was invited to their graduations but did not respond. Divorce is hard on the entire family, especially the kids. Taking out his frustrations on the kids in an attempt to hurt me only worked in the short term; in the long term, I predict he will regret treating his children in the manner that he did. Our son and daughter are now adults. Perhaps one day he will reach out to them if only to say hello and ask them how they are.

Chapter 5
RELOCATION

I had to enroll my daughter in her new school in Atlanta and, thanks to her lawyers teaching me the ropes in San Diego, I knew how to navigate her IEP like a pro. Tylar has always enjoyed school. Middle school (junior high school in San Diego) was typical. I worked nights and was able to visit her classroom and check on her progress. Tylar's middle school teacher was a good resource for me. He was truly interested in Tylar's progress. He wanted to see her win. You don't find teachers like him every day. I wished Tylar could have finished her school days with him, but alas she had to go to high school, and Salem High School proved to be by far her worst school years.

She was assigned to Salem High School, which I was against because of the distance from our home, and every time I was asked to pick her up from school it took me a while to reach the school. I was still working the night shift and I am thankful for that because I was constantly being called to the school to pick her up for reasons which seemed like the special education teacher and the paraprofessionals should have been able to resolve.

Tylar's high school teacher was a kind man named Mr. Roberts. He was at the end of his career and didn't want any conflict. He spoiled Tylar by giving in to her and letting her have her way. Unfortunately, on days when there was a substitute teacher, trouble always happened. Tylar is very used to routine and when Mr. Roberts was not there to provide that routine she would act out in school. The paraprofessionals were of little help. They were older, kind women who wanted their days to be uneventful. They did not take the job to advocate for the children. They would whisper their criticisms out of earshot of the administration.

The high school liked to pre-write Tylar's IEPs and when I arrived at the meeting I would insist every goal be re-written. My job as a mother is to make sure she is educated to the best of her ability, not just rubber stamped and passed through the system. In Georgia, special needs kids are able to stay in school until they are 22 years old and by the time my daughter was 22 I was thrilled it was over. Unfortunately, I kept Tylar at home a lot of her last year of high school. Between her being suspended for reasons that she couldn't comprehend and the overall ugly behavior of the school administration, it was easier and far more peaceful to have her at home with me. Little did they know Tylar had everything she could want in her own home.

If there are any school officials reading this book, please understand that special needs children matter, their feelings get hurt, and they want to be included and accepted. They deserve to be treated with dignity and respect like all students at the school. Suspending a low-functioning person with autism has zero effect because they don't know what a suspension is and why. If you cannot embrace all students, perhaps another career choice would be best for you. I attend parent meetings, I am an advocate, and we see you. Please do better. For all those who work in the education field and do exceptional work, we see you as well and appreciate everything you do to make the lives of our children better through your teaching and kindness.

When my son Troy graduated from high school and left for college, Tylar missed him more than anyone realized, and she began pulling out her hair and urinating on herself. It was six months in before I was able to connect the dots between his leaving and her regression. She was really agitated that he was not at home. My son lived on campus, which was approximately two hours west of our home. I eventually had to relent and put her on adult diapers when she would urinate in school and on the bus and wet her clothes throughout the day. CARD had potty trained her but they did not operate in Atlanta. She continues to use adult diapers but she also urinates in the toilet so it's difficult to get her to use the toilet out of necessity because she is urinating now as a sensory habit. Tylar's big sensory stimulation issues are mostly solved with beads, which she has thousands of and always has with her. The beads comfort her. She plays with them all day. She has other sensory issues but they come and go, whereas the beads are her mainstay.

I applied for the Now/Comp waiver, which will help her afford a day program which I preferred to her attempting to go work. I did this because I do not think she has the capability to work and, while several individuals with autism are able to work and thrive in a workplace environment, I don't see that as an option for Tylar. I know she will never live on her own without help and I'm content to have her here with me. For the last year, Tylar has been at home with me every day. She attends respite on some weekends and she can go to respite for five days a couple times per year. Respite affords her the opportunity to spend time with her peers and it gives me time to spend on myself.

She helps me around the house and with my business to the best of her ability. My son and I are also her legal guardians. I don't know what her future holds. I continue to advocate for her. Autism isn't an easy thing. It's difficult and still just as heartbreaking as the day of her diagnosis. I still cry sometimes, but I have learned to laugh also. I do my best knowing sometimes my best isn't good enough. I will always experience days where I feel overwhelmed. There will always be days of stress. I know how to better deal with bad days than I did years ago, and my goal is to help other parents and caregivers to do the same.

Chapter 6
WHAT DOES CAREGIVING REALLY MEAN?

What does it mean to be a caregiver? A caregiver is someone who is actively engaged in providing care and needs to another such as a chronically ill, disabled, or aged family member or friend. A caregiver is someone who helps meet the special needs of others with or without pay and often at a great personal cost to their own career, finances, social life, and mental health. Often a caregiver finds themselves in this role with a lack of training, support, or compensation.

Chapter 7
CAREGIVING AND PARENTING

Distinguishing between my role as a Caregiver and as a Mother is impossible for me. Both roles meld together seamlessly in everything I do for my son and daughter and always have.

If anyone asks, "Who are you?" with regard to my daughter, I answer, "I'm her mother." I don't say, "I'm her caregiver and her mother." They quickly learn that Tylar lives at home with me and that I provide her care 24/7/365. For me, all of the caregiving I have provided to my son and daughter is parenting.

Even when I advocate for my daughter, I wear my mom hat. "On behalf of my daughter …" "As the mother of an adult daughter on the autism spectrum …" "I'm applying for…" etc. Caregiving and parenting are carefully interwoven in my existence, and when I tend to Tylar's needs I feel like a mom looking after her child, not like a caregiver.

I have asked myself, "Would I do all that I've done for my daughter, for a person, who was not my child?" I don't know. I know that I am, by nature and through experience with my children, a caregiver. And I have provided care to elders in my family, but not intimate, day to day, keeping them alive care. The ultimate compelling reason why I am a care provider is that I am a mother.

So I guess, for me, there is no difference between being a caregiver and parenting. However, all caregivers are not parents and everyone who has provided care has their own reasons for doing so. Some people have made the decision to become caregivers for family members or go into a profession that requires caregiving. Despite your reasons for being a caregiver, you still must take the decision seriously and take good care of yourself. Additionally, there are those who have made the decision to become caregivers only to find out that they do not make good caregivers and that the job may be more than they can handle.

Chapter 8
CAREGIVER STRESS

Caregiver stress is an effect of the emotional and physical strain of caregiving. Caregivers have much higher levels of stress than people who are not caregivers. Many caregivers are providing help or are "on call" almost all day. Some caregivers also work full-time jobs in addition to being caregivers. Sometimes, this means there is little time for sleep, self-care, or other family members or friends. Some caregivers may feel overwhelmed by the amount of care their aging, sick, or disabled family member needs. Anyone can fall victim to caregiver stress. Caring for a loved one who needs constant medical care and supervision can lead to many health problems and even depression. It's important to get regular screening, enough sleep, and exercise. You may think everything is okay, but caregiver stress can take many forms. For instance, you may feel frustrated and angry one minute and helpless the next. You may make mistakes when giving medicines. Or you may turn to unhealthy behaviors like smoking or drinking too much alcohol.

Other signs and symptoms include:

- Feeling overwhelmed
- Feeling alone, isolated, or deserted by others
- Sleeping too much or too little
- Gaining or losing a lot of weight
- Feeling tired most of the time
- Losing interest in activities you used to enjoy
- Becoming easily irritated or angered
- Feeling worried or sad often
- Having headaches or body aches often

Talk to your doctor about your symptoms and ways to relieve stress. Also, let others give you a break. Reach out to family, friends, or a local resource.

Some stress can be good for you, as it helps you cope and respond to a change or challenge. But the long-term stress of any kind, including caregiver stress, can lead to serious health problems.

Some of the ways stress affects caregivers include:

Depression and anxiety. Anxiety and depression also raise your risk for other health problems, such as heart disease and stroke.

Weak immune system. Stressed caregivers may have weaker immune systems.

Obesity. Stress causes weight gain. Obesity raises your risk for other health problems, including heart disease and stroke.

Higher risk for chronic diseases. High levels of stress, especially when combined with depression, can raise your risk for health problems, such as heart disease, cancer, diabetes, or arthritis.

Taking steps to relieve caregiver stress helps prevent health problems. Also, taking care of yourself helps you take better care of your loved one and enjoy the rewards of caregiving.

Here are some tips to help you prevent or manage caregiver stress:

Learn ways to better help your loved one. Some hospitals offer classes that can teach you how to care for someone with an injury or illness. To find these classes, ask your doctor.

Find caregiving resources in your community to help you. Many communities have adult daycare services or respite services to give primary caregivers a break from their caregiving duties. My daughter attends respite camps and weekends throughout the year.

Ask for and accept help. Make a list of ways others can help you. Let helpers choose what they would like to do. For instance, someone might sit with the person you care for while you do an errand. Someone else might pick up groceries for you. Get out of the mindset that you must do everything.

Join a support group for caregivers. You can find a general caregiver support group or a group of caregivers who care for someone with the same illness or disability as your loved one. You can share stories, pick up caregiving tips, and get support from others who face the same challenges as you do. I belong to more than one, and my best resource is other parents with autistic children. I also moderate a Facebook group named "Caregiving Life," which you are welcome to join. It's a closed group so you can feel free to openly share with others with no judgment. Simply click "join" and you will be added to the group.

Get organized. Make to-do lists and set a daily routine. I plan for tomorrow the night before. Plan meals for the week.

Take time for yourself. Stay in touch with family and friends and do things you enjoy with your loved ones. This is a must. You have to continue to live your life.

Take care of your health. Find time to be physically active on most days of the week, choose healthy foods, and get enough sleep.

See your doctor for regular checkups. Make sure to tell your doctor or nurse you are a caregiver. Also, tell her about any symptoms of depression or sickness you may have. Doctors cannot help you if you don't ask. Ask.

If you work outside the home and are feeling overwhelmed, consider taking a break from your job. Under the federal Family and Medical Leave Act, eligible employees can take up to 12 weeks of unpaid leave per year to care for relatives. Ask your human resources office about your options. I cannot tell you how many days I have taken off, harassment-free, under this law. FMLA is not just to care for a loved, one but it's also in place for you to take self-care days.

Although caregiving can be very challenging, it also has its rewards. It feels good to be able to care for a loved one. Spending time together can give new meaning to your relationship.

Remember that you need to take care of yourself to be able to care for your loved one, and sometimes that means saying "no" to people and things that do not serve that purpose.

Chapter 9
FINANCIAL STRESS

Financial caregiving is a complex series of tasks. The best way to approach it is step-by-step and by being an organized caregiver. Knowing things are "good to go" when the time comes that a loved one needs help will make the transition much easier and less stressful for the caregiver and loved one alike.

If you are a caregiver that is helping an aging loved one manage their money, this can be added stress, especially if they do not have all their financial life in order. Hopefully, they have enough money to cover their expenses, but often this is not the case. Do not dismiss the benefit of pre-planning and being prepared. Discussions about money can be difficult and if you have other family members that want to help out, a family meeting should be called. If you prepare, you can have a family meeting earlier before everyone is emotional and stressed out. You will need to discuss budgeting and planning for the future. There are a number of things to consider when preparing to take on another's finances, in any capacity. A caregiver must not let their own anxiety, or even guilt, influence decisions on their loved one's behalf. It's essential he or she allow their loved one to retain their independence and feel included in decisions, if possible.

My daughter does not have the capacity to make her own financial decisions even though she receives a Social Security check each month. My son and I long ago became her legal guardians. She has her own bank accounts and we basically make financial decisions that are to her benefit. She does choose what she wants to buy, with our guidance. If a loved one is completely unable to participate in their financial plan, a caregiver must make every effort to involve all immediate family members. Nothing causes sibling rivalry faster than one brother or sister who feels left out and unappreciated. Each may have a unique perspective and personal experience to supplement the planning process, and every voice deserves to be heard. Family meetings, whether in person or telephone, are a great way to keep everyone informed on spending and bank balances. Even though it is more efficient for one person to be keeping the checkbook and assets up to date, many siblings would be more than happy to help out if asked. As a caregiver, a team effort is vital. This way, should a crisis happen to strike, all parties are on the same page, ready to respond. It is important to have a backup plan in the event the primary caregiver becomes incapacitated so the other person can step right in without any disruption.

A CAREGIVERS CHECKLIST

Practice fiscal responsibility

It is imperative a person of any age live within their means. If you see reckless spending from the person you are caring for don't be shy; bring up the conversation even though it's difficult.

Know where to find important documents

A loved one's will or trust is the most obvious document families may think to have access to. Though wills are essential, there are many other documents a financial caregiver needs. Insurance policies, mortgage records, retirement records, and bank statements are just a few. A caregiver should take time to locate these as soon as possible, in the event of an emergency.

Passwords

You will need usernames and passwords to access online accounts. It is an absolute necessity that a financial caregiver gain complete access to their loved one's funds and assets. He or she may need to become a joint owner of an account or make arrangements through the financial institution to be able to conduct transactions, but do not make this decision on your own. Many a family has been torn apart by one person taking over without at least talking to other family members. The ability to quickly access information will not only protect a loved one's assets during an emergency, but it will also eliminate frustration down the road. Don't forget to ask about email addresses and their passwords, house alarm passwords, and codes.

Automate everything you can

A caregiver can easily set up monthly debits from a loved one's checking to pay utilities, insurance, mortgage bills, etc. The payment will most likely be linked to an email address, which allows a caregiver to see when payments are made, and ensures they are. If the person you are caring for receives Social Security or retirement checks, direct deposit is mandatory nowadays and it's easier than going to the bank to cash checks.

Anticipate future expenses

Once access to accounts and bill payments are set up, a caregiver should look to the future and anticipate what's to come. Take an inventory of assets versus debts to determine a loved one's actual net worth. In addition to medical services, living expenses may change frequently. A good caregiver, however, knows to always be prepared for both the expected and the unexpected, and you never know what tomorrow may bring.

GET YOUR PAPERS IN ORDER

In addition to gaining full access to financial records, there is other paperwork you need to fill out in the event a loved one is unable to care for themselves. Hopefully, they already have a will in place. You may need to consider

Power of Attorney and a Living Will. A Living Will allows a caregiver to make health care decisions for the person in the event they are unable to do so themselves. You should check to see if they have a "Do Not Resuscitate Order" in place also. Locate any life insurance policies, auto insurance policies, and social security information. Ideally, they will have already expressed what they would like to happen. As I wrote above, my son and I already have guardianship of my daughter, so we can make the necessary financial and healthcare decisions. Obtaining guardianship is not free, and there is a court proceeding involved. This can be expensive. If you are prepared in advance it will save you a lot of stress.

TAKING CARE OF YOU

Caring for another is a large responsibility, especially since many caregivers are near or at retirement age themselves. Caregivers should have a personal financial plan in place, as well as another plan drawn up for their loved one. A good plan includes a monthly budget with expenses and income listed, review of health insurance plan(s) and what is covered, and assessment of assets and debt. As for myself, I do not have to create a budget for my daughter even though she has separate accounts. I do, however, keep her accounts balanced and in good standing. You can find resources online to print out budget sheets or you can track and input your budget online if it's more convenient.

Caregivers should also contact their tax adviser or the Internal Revenue Service to find out what deductions may be available to them. If providing full-time care to a loved one, it may be possible to claim that person as a dependent. I claim my daughter, as I always have, even though she is an adult. There are deductions you may qualify for depending on your caregiver status. Don't make assumptions; check with a tax adviser.

DON'T GO IT ALONE

Many resources are available for caregivers dealing with a loved one's financial issues. The first sector is private, which includes bankers, lawyers, insurance agents, and financial planners. These people may have had dealings with a loved one in the past and have a detailed knowledge of their finances.

Some other private professionals specialize in helping the ill or elderly. Elder law attorneys handle estate planning, Medicare and Medicaid issues, fraud, and other legal issues. Daily money managers may assist in paying bills, balancing a checkbook, and monitoring daily financial issues. They are a good resource for long-distance caregivers. So are geriatric care managers, a growing profession that I personally did not know existed until recently. These professionals assist families in whatever capacity is needed, including financial management.

Second, public resources are available. Social service agencies are sponsored by state or county governments and have aging resources for residents. From the Social Security office to local government programs, many groups are established to help caregivers provide the best care possible and be organized in the process.

RAISE Family Caregivers Act (Recognize, Assist, Include, Support, and Engage)

A new law will require the federal government to develop a national strategy to address the needs of family caregivers, including those supporting people with developmental disabilities.

The law calls for the secretary of health and human services to establish a national plan to "recognize and support family caregivers" within 18 months (from January 2018). The plan is supposed to include recommendations for federal, state, and local governments, as well as health care and long-term services and supports providers. The strategy is to be updated every other year.

Additionally, the legislation also creates a family caregiving advisory council comprised of federal officials and stakeholders in the community to guide the strategy's development and advise the secretary and other members of government on how to support the more than 40 million family caregivers across the country.

The RAISE Act is new as of the writing of this book so, although it is too soon for us to see the benefits it will bring, I am confident that this bill will help caregivers continue in their much-needed roles with more support. The goals of the strategy include identifying actions that government, communities, health providers, employers, and others can take to support family caregivers, including:

- Promoting greater adoption of person-centered care and family-centered care in health settings and long-term care settings
- Training for family caregivers
- Respite options for family caregivers
- Ways to increase financial security for family caregivers
- Workplace policies to help family caregivers keep working
- Collecting and sharing of information about innovative family caregiving models
- Assessing federal programs around family caregiving
- Addressing disparities and meeting the needs of the diverse caregiving population

Only time will tell if the RAISE Act truly makes a difference. I like to see the world through positive eyes, so my guess is that it will.

Chapter 10
TAKE CARE OR BURN OUT

Caregiver burnout is a state of physical, emotional, and mental exhaustion that may be accompanied by a change in attitude — from positive and caring to negative and unconcerned. Burnout can occur when caregivers don't get the help they need, or if they try to do more than they are able — either physically or financially. Caregivers who are "burned out" may experience fatigue, stress, anxiety, and depression. Many caregivers also feel guilty if they spend time on themselves rather than on their disabled, ill, or elderly loved ones.

I am all too familiar with caregiver burnout. Most of my burnout symptoms show up as irritability, hopelessness, and depression. I've never shared my burnout voluntarily with my family members other than my son because, honestly, there was nothing they could do to help anyway. Sure, they could make suggestions and listen, but what I needed was a break, and people making suggestions about things they were not in a position to implement, while well-meaning, did nothing to help my situation. My son is my lifesaver. He understands autism and we have both helped each other when my daughter has been uncontrollable. I also stay aware that he doesn't fall victim to burnout. I appreciate his help, but I don't want to ask him for more than he is able to provide, so I make sure he is living a full life and pursuing his dreams. I can only imagine how life for him growing up with an autistic sister felt. I think siblings are often overlooked when it comes to needing help to cope. My son and I have and still do talk about how he feels about his sister. Over the years there have been many parents who have thrown in the towel and committed murder/suicide because of burnout, and all you hear on the news is about this horrible mother or this horrible father and how could they do such a thing?

To lose hope can throw you into the depths of depression. To not see any light at the end of the tunnel is a horrible thing. It would be nice if some of the people hanging on these news stories could have offered to babysit, cook a meal, offer the family some time to relax. I don't have all the answers, but I do know how it feels to be depressed, hopeless, and **helpless.**

What Are the Symptoms of Caregiver Burnout?

The symptoms of caregiver burnout are similar to the symptoms of stress and depression. They may include:

- Withdrawal from friends and family
- Loss of interest in activities previously enjoyed

- Feeling blue, irritable, hopeless, and helpless
- Changes in appetite, weight, or both
- Changes in sleep patterns
- Getting sick more often
- Feelings of wanting to hurt yourself or the person for whom you are caring
- Emotional and physical exhaustion
- Excessive use of alcohol and/or sleep medications
- Irritability

What Causes Caregiver Burnout?

Caregivers often are so busy caring for others that they tend to neglect their own emotional, mental and physical health. The demands on a caregiver's body, mind, and emotions can easily seem overwhelming, leading to fatigue and hopelessness — and, ultimately, burnout. Other factors that can lead to caregiver burnout include:

- **Unrealistic expectations** — Many caregivers expect their involvement to have a positive effect on the health and happiness of the patient. This may be unrealistic for patients suffering from a progressive disease, such as Parkinson's or Alzheimer's. If you are the parent of a child with autism on the lower end of the spectrum and choose to be a caregiver, you must realize there is no cure and that you will be a lifelong caregiver.
- **Lack of control** —- Many caregivers become frustrated by a lack of money, resources, and skills to effectively plan, manage, and organize their loved one's care.

- **Unreasonable demands** — Some caregivers place unreasonable burdens upon themselves, in part because they see providing care as their exclusive responsibility. Asking for help is asking for a lifeline. Don't be too prideful.
- **Other factors** — Many caregivers cannot recognize when they are suffering burnout and eventually get to the point where they cannot function effectively. They may even become sick themselves. The best thing you can do for yourself is to seek help. Caregiving can be a full-time job, and if you are also working a full-time job you have to recognize the signs of burnout before it's too late.

How Can I Prevent Caregiver Burnout?

Here are some steps you can take to help prevent caregiver burnout:

- Find someone you trust — such as a friend, co-worker, or neighbor — to talk to about your feelings and frustrations. There are several online forums where you can communicate with other caregivers and exchange information.
- Set realistic goals, accept that you may need help with caregiving, and turn to others for help with some tasks. This is critical. You do a disservice to yourself, as well as the person you are taking care of if you insist on trying to do everything yourself.

- Be realistic about your loved one's disease, especially if it is a progressive disease such as Parkinson's or Alzheimer's.
- Don't forget about yourself because you're too busy caring for someone else. Set aside time for yourself, even if it's just an hour or two. Remember, taking care of yourself is not a luxury; it is an absolute necessity if you're going to be an effective caregiver.
- Talk to a professional. Most therapists, social workers, and clergy members are trained to counsel individuals dealing with a wide range of physical and emotional issues.
- Take advantage of respite care services. Respite care provides a temporary break for caregivers. This can range from a few hours of in-home care to a short stay in a nursing home or assisted living facility. My daughter attends respite weekends almost monthly. This gives me a break.
- Know your limits and do a reality check of your personal situation. Recognize and accept your potential for caregiver burnout.
- Educate yourself. The more you know about the illness, the more effective you will be in caring for the person with the illness. I continually educate myself on autism issues.
- Develop new tools for coping. Remember to lighten up and accentuate the positive. Use humor to help deal with everyday stresses.
- Stay healthy by eating right and getting plenty of exercise and sleep.

- Accept your feelings. Having negative feelings — such as frustration or anger — about your responsibilities or the person for whom you are caring is normal. It does not mean you are a bad person or a bad caregiver. I've cried about my feelings on many occasions. I'm sure there will be more tears in the years to come.

Where can you turn for help with caregiver burnout?

If you are already suffering from stress and depression, seek medical attention. Stress and depression are treatable disorders. If you want to help prevent burnout, consider turning to the following resources for help with your caregiving:

- **Home health services** — These agencies provide home health aides and nurses for short-term care if your loved one is acutely ill. Some agencies provide short-term respite care.
- **Adult day care** — These programs offer a place for seniors to socialize, engage in a variety of activities, and receive needed medical care and other services.
- **Nursing homes or assisted living facilities** — These institutions sometimes offer short-term respite stays to provide caregivers a break from their caregiving responsibilities.
- **Private care aides** — These are professionals who specialize in assessing current needs and

coordinating care and services. Be prepared to pay for this service.

• **Caregiver support services** — These include support groups and other programs that can help caregivers recharge their batteries, meet others coping with similar issues, find more information, and locate additional resources.

Chapter 11
TAKE CARE OR DEPRESSION

Caregiver depression can take a toll on you and your ability to care for your loved one. Understand the signs of caregiver depression — and know how to prevent it. Caregiving is often physically and emotionally stressful. While you are trying to provide the best care possible, you might put your loved one's needs before your own. In turn, you could develop feelings of sadness, anger, and loneliness. Sometimes, these emotions can trigger caregiver depression.

Caregiving alone does not cause depression, nor will everyone who provides care experience the negative feelings that go with depression. But in an effort to provide the best possible care for a family member or friend, caregivers often sacrifice physical and emotional needs, and the emotional and physical experiences involved with providing care can strain even the most capable person. The resulting feelings of anger, anxiety, sadness, isolation, exhaustion — and then guilt for having these feelings — can take a heavy toll on even the strongest people.

Caregiving is hard; it can lead to feelings of stress, guilt, anger, sadness, isolation — and depression. Depression affects different people in different ways and at different times. For example, I experienced depression right after my daughter was diagnosed with autism. Other caregivers may experience depression once they realize there is not a cure for certain ailments, and watching their loved ones slowly decline is very depressing.

Signs and symptoms of depression include:

- Becoming easily agitated or frustrated
- Feelings of worthlessness or guilt
- Feelings of hopelessness
- Thoughts of death, dying, or suicide
- Disturbed sleep
- Fatigue or loss of energy
- Loss of interest or pleasure in usual activities
- Difficulty thinking or concentrating
- Changes in appetite and weight
- Physical symptoms that do not respond to treatment, such as headaches, digestive disorders, and pain

Recognizing that the stress you are experiencing can sometimes lead to depression is the first step to preventing it — and burnout. To take that step, talk about your feelings, frustrations, and fears with your doctor and ask for a referral for a mental health professional. Talking helps you understand what's going on for you and for the person in your care. It helps you come to grips with the fact that you are not in total control of the situation.

Early attention to symptoms of depression may help to prevent the development of a more serious depression over time. Some suggestions are:

- Set realistic goals in light of the depression and assume a reasonable amount of responsibility. Taking on more than you can handle only sets you up for failure.
- Break large tasks into small ones, set some priorities, and do what you can as you can.
- Try to be with other people and to confide in someone; it is usually better than being alone and secretive.
- Participate in activities that may make you feel better, such as mild exercise, going to a movie, or getting a massage. Going to church and social events gives you the opportunity to get out of the house and be with other people.
- Expect your mood to improve gradually, not immediately. Feeling better takes time.
- People rarely "snap out of" a depression but they can feel a little better day by day. Keep a journal and write down your feelings.
- Remember, positive thinking will replace the negative thinking that is part of the depression. The

negative thinking will be reduced as your depression responds to treatment.
- Let your family and friends help you.

Chapter 12
TAKE CARE
TO EAT BETTER

Why do we reach for the chips and chocolate when our day begins to spiral out of control? It's because they have a temporary calming effect on the body, research shows. But they're also unhealthy and, as a caregiver, the last thing you need is to undermine your health by eating poorly. So it's important to understand why "comfort" eating makes you feel better and also how to keep it under control.

Studies suggest that the stress response system plays a role in how we crave foods and store energy. When the body is under stress, the neurochemicals that help balance our moods do not function properly and the body releases stress hormones. These stress hormones cause cravings for high-sugar and high-fat foods. Overconsumption of these foods can lead to an increased amount of fat being stored in the abdomen. And the added weight gain puts you at higher risk for high blood pressure, heart disease, and diabetes. Most people have a trigger point when it comes to stress. A single unexpected incident can upset the rhythm of your day, triggering an emotional outburst that often sends you to the nearest container of ice cream, a bar of chocolate, or bag of chips for comfort. I tend to reach for all three.

How can you learn what triggers your emotional overeating and understand how to address it in a healthy way? First, become more aware of situations that upset you, and examine how they make you feel. Then, think about how and why the foods you eat make you feel better. From there, work on finding alternative ways to deal with those situations when they arise. Here are a few suggestions:

- Talk with a friend or a family member about your feelings as a release for your emotions, rather than eating.

- Keep a journal to record your feelings when you're tempted to overeat.

- When you feel you can't overcome your stress-related overeating alone, seek professional counsel to assist you.

- Get regular physical activity, like walking or yoga, to release stress and displace eating time.

Following any of these tips or suggestions or developing your own plan will help you recognize stressful situations so you can deal with an issue in a positive manner that doesn't necessarily include running to the refrigerator.

Keep healthy foods handy

Some foods can actually help your body repair itself from stress damage and also reduce cravings for high-sugar and salty snacks. The trick is to make healthy foods accessible and ready to eat. If it helps, you can buy healthy foods in bulk so they are there instead of junk food. Keep a bowl of apples, oranges, and bananas on the kitchen counter and keep bite-sized veggies and nuts such as carrots, raisins, and pecans nearby for you to grab when you need a quick snack. These healthy choices not only help satisfy your immediate "need to eat," but also offer important nutrients. Here are a variety of nutritious fruits, vegetables, and nuts to choose from:

- Oranges, strawberries, broccoli, spinach, and peppers are high in Vitamin C

- Whole grains such as brown rice, whole grain bread or leafy green vegetables have plenty of B vitamins

- Almonds, whole grains, and sunflower seeds are high in magnesium

- Walnuts and flaxseeds are rich in omega-3 oils

Listen to your body

As your loved one's primary caregiver, it's important to recognize how you're feeling both physically and mentally every day. Chronic stress can have a negative impact on you and, in turn, can compromise the level of care you provide. So, the bottom line is "Take care of yourself." Get the counsel and support you need to help manage your stress and make smart, healthy food choices regularly, so you're feeling your best as you care for your loved one. When you stop making poor food choices your body will thank you, and the response will be immediate.

Chapter 13
TAKE CARE BY EXERCISING MORE

Caregivers have little spare time for themselves. So, when you do get a break, you're probably craving rest, rather than thinking of exercise. Yet, of the two, exercise could be a far better choice. It may prevent you from getting sick, help you sleep better, and is almost certain to give you more energy, definitely something of prime importance to a caregiver.

Your well-being can affect the quality of care you provide to your loved one; I know this firsthand. Research has found that caregivers are more vulnerable to illness and can get sicker if they don't take care of themselves. If you already have an exercise routine that you have been doing, please keep it up. If not, here are a few steps to get started.

Start simple

Going to the gym may be attractive, but it may not be realistic if you squander precious time on packing appropriate clothes, traveling to and from the gym, and arranging alternative care for your loved one while you're there.

Instead, you can keep exercise as simple as a brisk walk around the block. I recommend not thinking big. Just take a walk, and if you like podcasts or music then pop on a headset and walk. I always listen to business and motivational podcasts when I exercise, which is walking more often than not. Caregivers are often overwhelmed from a busy workday, so just walking as exercise may be the most they can do. Believe me, it's better than not doing anything. It's a great release and way to be alone, recharge, meditate, and collect oneself. I use an app on my phone to count my steps so I can track my daily steps. I have a daily goal of 10,500 steps. Don't think of this as exercise. Many studies have demonstrated that regular walking is one of the best things you can do to improve physical and mental health.

Another option is to use exercise at home. Your loved one may be able to sit on the couch and watch you work out, or you can try to schedule your exercise during nap time or when he or she is otherwise occupied. You can find plenty of exercise videos and instruction on YouTube. Sometimes I take my daughter on walks with me, and I have seen parents/caregivers with their children exercising with them as well.

Get enough

Exercise recommendations are much the same for anyone. Your goal should be 30 to 40 minutes of moderately intense exercise at least three times a week.

Ideally, you'll want to exercise continuously for 30 minutes or more. (Some research says this gives you the maximum benefit.) However, taking that much time off may not be an option unless you have help.

It's okay to get your exercise here and there throughout the day. Research shows that even little bursts of activity are beneficial. Park the car farther away from the grocery store to get some extra steps in or take the stairs instead of the elevator. Build up to more time as you begin to see and feel the benefits of exercise.

Your exercise goals may include losing weight or toning certain body parts. Or you may be seeking to release stress and regain energy, stamina, and strength. Try to get the most from the time you exercise. When you take a walk you should move briskly to get your heart rate elevated. You should feel that you've exerted yourself a bit. Working up a sweat is one way to tell that you are getting a good workout. Another clue is to listen to your breathing — it should become shorter, but you should be able to hold a conversation. If you can't have a conversation (even with yourself), slow down. And, remember, check with a health professional before beginning any exercise program. You can buy exercise mats and inexpensive lightweight equipment such as kettle-bells, dumb-bells, or jump ropes to get yourself moving. You will notice the difference once you get started.

Chapter 14
TAKE CARE SLEEP MORE

I have a hard time getting a good night's sleep. My daughter has sleep problems, so by default, I have sleep problems. I worked the night shift for 34 years of my 35-year career. While working nights helped me be available for my kids, it ruined my sleep. Now that I'm retired I still have a hard time sleeping because my daughter does not have a regular sleep pattern. I get my best sleep when I take a break from caregiving while my daughter attends respite. A good night's sleep is one of the most basic yet elusive things we need for our health and well-being as caregivers. Hands down my biggest frustration is losing so much sleep. I never know when my daughter will wake up or go to sleep. On good days I am able to plan my morning before she wakes. On bad days she may have already been up for a couple hours.

The stress of not being able to get good sleep causes a headache, shoulder pains, chest pains, and feelings of hopelessness. Additionally, I worry about her lack of sleep and the seizures that can happen as a result, not to mention the damage she is doing to our home during this time.

When I worked full-time I would go to work in zombie mode. I've had to take pills to keep me awake in order to drive home safely. Sleep is important. It's not always possible, but try to get as much sleep as you can. If your sleep is routinely disrupted by the person you are caring for, it's important that you plan to get more sleep. Sleeping poorly increases your risk for health problems. Sleep deprivation can lead to high blood pressure, heart disease, diabetes, stroke, and obesity. You could very well end up being the person who needs care rather than the provider. If you are feeling exhausted, please make your own sleep a priority and seek help.

Chapter 15

TAKE CARE OF THE F-WORD: FRUSTRATION

No matter how much we love the person we are caring for, caregiving can be frustrating. Think about the big picture. If you're frustrated with the person you are caring for, imagine things from their perspective. I know my daughter sometimes can't help her behavior and gets frustrated when people can't understand her and that must feel terrible, so I think about how it must be to live with autism. Remember, it's okay to be upset. Being frustrated doesn't make you a bad caregiver or a bad person. It just makes you human.

Frustration just comes with the package. We're human, and caregiving inevitably involves situations and tasks that are inherently frustrating. So many of us feel guilty for losing our cool, but it happens to even the most patient caregiver, eventually. It's okay to get frustrated. It will happen. Frustration is a normal part of being a caregiver. It's how you cope with it that will keep you as the caregiver and not the one needing care. If you can, take a break. You probably can't take the day off or even get an hour's peace. You can hopefully step into another space for a minute to take a deep breath and clear your head. Even though I consider myself a very patient person, I frequently become frustrated. My daughter doesn't have the type of autism you may see in the feel-good stories on the news. She isn't high functioning; she is on the lower end of the spectrum, so she won't become a team captain or be able to work a job. She pulls out her hair and hits herself in the head. She removes her fingernails and cuts up her clothes to use the material to mix with her beads. She has zero sense of danger and will need caregiving and direction for the rest of her life. Even with practicing self-care and utilizing respite on some weekends, when my daughter is home there is no real break or support when she has insomnia, seizures, and mental breakdown. Frustration can be a daily challenge. I understand that frustration will be a part of my life because I choose to keep my daughter home with me rather than place her in a facility. Everyone should know their frustration triggers because something that frustrates you may not bother me at all. Know what frustrates you so you can best handle the situation.

Situations that frustrate me and how I handle them are:

Constant interruptions

My daughter wants what she wants when she wants it. When she wakes up she is ready to eat, so rather than wait until she wakes up I get up before her and put her cereal in a bowl, pour her juice, and get her morning medications ready. I put her toothpaste on her toothbrush, place her towel, washcloth, and soap near the bathtub. While she is in the tub I lay out her clothes for the day. If I have everything ready to go I feel less frustration and I can begin work on things I want to accomplish for the day. My daughter likes to overeat, so I make sure to lock the fridge and cabinets before I go to bed at night.

I have a home-based business that I need to work on daily, so I try to anticipate her wants so she doesn't become agitated and have a meltdown. If she has a meltdown, it disrupts my thoughts and creative flow and my productivity is ruined for the day, so I lay out all the things she needs to keep herself busy for a couple of hours while I'm working. Part of it requires cultivating your overall resilience. The more resilient we are, the easier we can rebalance after something throws us off.

Chapter 16

ISOLATION

I'm not always able to have friends over to my house, mainly because my daughter may come streaking through the family room naked on any given day. She may decide she wants to sniff people on Tuesday or spit on people the next day. I usually do not mind explaining her behavior to anyone, but sometimes I am embarrassed and sometimes I'm fed up. I become frustrated and caught up in my own thoughts of bitterness and sadness with the realization that I walk this path alone behind closed doors. My family and friends do the best they can to muster up the offers to help, mostly from a sense of obligation, but in the end, I rarely take them up on their offers because it's hard for me and I'm her mother, so it would be doubly hard on them. When people have not walked in your shoes it's easy for them to second guess everything you do, and I have found that keeping my mouth shut has worked wonders in some cases. Sometimes it's an isolating life. Find your people, find your tribe, surround yourself with people who get you, and connect with others when possible to relieve the feelings of isolation. Know that you are not alone in this walk.

Chapter 17
TAKE CARE OF GUILT

"Did I do something to cause my daughter to have autism? Am I being punished for something I have done? Did I work too much? Was it something I ate? Did I take care of myself when I was pregnant? I remember thinking that perhaps she was deprived of something by my having a C-section. Maybe I should have started prenatal vitamins earlier. Surely, this must be my fault. Much self-reproach and remorse can stem from questioning the causes of the disability.

Guilt feelings may also be manifested in historical religious interpretations. Questioning God and asking, "Why, Lord?" is all too common when a child has a disability. Although feeling guilty is normal, it still feels bad, often fueled by the expectations of others or the expectations you place on yourself. Guilt can weigh you down and become a burden. When I drop my daughter off for respite I still feel guilty after all these years. I know that her going to respite allows her to spend time with her peers and it allows me time to de-stress, but I still have feelings of guilt every time. Everyone experiences guilt because it often arises when there's a mismatch between your day-today choices and the choices the "perfect you" would have made. The "perfect you" may be the caregiver who indulges every whim of people at the sacrifice of your own needs, and when you finally do something for yourself you feel as though you're falling short.

You may have needs out of line with this "perfect you." You may believe that your own needs are insignificant, compared to the needs of your sick loved one. You then feel guilty when you even recognize your needs, much less act upon them. A mother may ask herself, "How can I go out for a walk with my kids when my mother is at home in pain?" (A hint for this mother: she can give more to her mother with an open heart when she takes good care of herself.)

You may have feelings misaligned with the "perfect you." Feeling angry about the injustice of your loved one's illness? You might even feel angry at your loved one for getting sick! Recognizing those feelings can produce a healthy dose of guilt. Yes, you may even feel guilty about feeling guilty.

If you're the kind of person prone to guilt, learn to manage guilt so that guilt serves you rather than imprisons you. Here are eight tips for managing your caregiver guilt:

Recognize the feeling of guilt: Unrecognized guilt eats at your soul. Name it; look at the monster under the bed. I didn't recognize my feelings of guilt until another parent pointed it out to me.

Identify other feelings: Often, there are feelings under the feeling of guilt. Name those, too. For example, say to yourself: "I hate to admit this to myself, but I'm resentful that (insert name) illness changed all of our lives." Once you put it into words, you will have a new perspective. You will also be reminding yourself of how fortunate you are to have what it takes to take care of loved one.

Be compassionate with yourself: Cloudy moods, like cloudy days, come and go. There's no one way a caregiver should feel. When you give yourself permission to have any feeling and recognize that your feelings don't control your actions, your guilt will subside.

Look for the cause of the guilt: What is the mismatch between this "perfect you" and the real you? Do you have an unmet need? Do you need to change your actions so that they align with your values?

Take action: Meet your needs. Needs are not bad or good; they just are. If you need some time alone, find someone to be with your loved one.

Change your behavior to fit your values: For example, Beverly felt guilty because her friend was in the hospital and she didn't send a card. Her guilt propelled her to buy some beautiful blank cards to make it easier for her to drop a note the next time.

Ask for help: Call a friend and say, "I'm going through a hard time. Do you have a few minutes just to listen?" Have a family meeting and say, "Our lives have been a lot different since Grandma got sick. I'm spending more time with her. Let's figure out together how we'll get everything done."

Revisit and reinvent the "perfect you": You made the best choices based on your resources and knowledge at the time. As you look to the future, you can create a refined vision of the "perfect you." What legacy do you want to leave? What values do you hold dear? Then, when you wake up in the morning and put on your clothes, imagine dressing the "perfect you." Let this reinvented "perfect you" make those moment-to-moment choices that create your legacy.

Understand that you will be a more effective caregiver when you care for the caregiver first. Loved ones neither want nor expect you to be a selfless servant. As a caregiver, when you care about yourself, you increase and improve your level of care. Yes, guilt is part of caregiving, but this guilt can help you become the caregiver you and your loved one want you to be.

Chapter 18
Set Boundaries, Say No

It took me a while to learn the art of saying NO, but now that I have I consider it a survival skill. It was not a simple thing for me to learn because I grew up believing I needed to explain myself or explain the situation, circumstances, the reason for saying "no." Saying "yes" tends to be entwined with being a good person and not feeling guilty. But the price is huge, more so for caregivers. As a caregiver, it's essential that you become an expert in setting boundaries. Boundaries are the flip side of asking for help. And if you can do both … if you can learn to say, "No" and "I need your help," you might just survive this experience.

It's all well and good for caregiving experts to say, "Make sure you take care of yourself," but they skip a step when they give this advice. Because let me tell you this: It's impossible to take care of yourself if you don't have good boundaries.

But just in case you're like I used to be, and you have a problem with boundaries, allow me to tell you the benefits of setting boundaries. Prior to the death of my father, I visited a behavioral health specialist because I was exhausted. I was not only physically tired, I was also mentally and emotionally spent. What I learned from that doctor is that the condition I was in was a direct result of not having boundaries. I had spent a good portion of my adult life making sure that everyone else was okay and not making sure that I was okay. I had a problem saying "no" and for that reason I became to "go to" person for everyone else's needs. Taking care of everyone else in addition to raising my children plus being a caregiver became far too much for me. My life was spiraling out control. It took me going to see a doctor and having him tell me I had to set boundaries and learn to say NO.

People will test your boundaries, and if you do not have any in place they will continue to push them. You have the right to decline a request that does fit into your daily agenda. You have the right to say no. I'm not saying you have to say no in a rude way, but you can politely and firmly decline. This may seem obvious on the surface, but you'd be surprised how many of us feel like we have to say yes to every ask and feel drained of energy afterward. I've noticed my own tendency to say yes and immediately become resentful of the person asking because I did not know how to say no; I did not have boundaries in place.

Because of my having several productive appointments with a psychologist, I am now fiercely protective of my time. Instead of telling people what I won't do I now tell them what I can do. The good thing about this is it keeps the peace and limits the request. The next time someone asks you to do something that you can't or don't want to do, just try thinking about what you can do, even if it's less than or different from the original ask and offer that as your response. People may become upset with you in the beginning, but as time goes on they will respect your decisions. You are only one person and you must take care to give care.

Chapter 19
FIND A HOBBY

I think everyone needs a hobby, especially caregivers. I am fortunate to have a hobby that my daughter enjoys and one that I turned into a business. I love jigsaw puzzles and have assembled hundreds of jigsaw puzzles that I proudly display on the walls of my garage (you can see pics at puzzlebilities.com). Jigsaw puzzle assembly has many benefits, stress relieving being one of the many. A hobby can help you to have something fun to look forward to doing each day, help you to clear your mind, and help you to develop a new skill which can lead to higher self-esteem. Even though your days as a caregiver are hectic and busy, it is well worth it to carve out a little time for hobbies, as it can save you from toxic stress in the long run, and even caregiver burnout. For those interested in trying out a new hobby or activity, here are just a few examples to help give you an idea of where to begin.

Crafting

Crafting is a fun and creative activity that can help you to brighten up your day. For those who love the idea of preserving memories, scrapbooking can be a great craft to learn. Not only will you be able to unwind as you design and create pages, you will be creating a keepsake heirloom for future generations. For those who don't enjoy the precision, cutting, and pasting of scrapbooking, there are crafts such as knitting and crocheting which are easy to learn and relaxing to do. In addition, your creations may be very useful to yourself and your loved ones!

Trying a New Physical Activity

When it comes to lowering stress, nearly nothing is more effective than exercise. However, exercising does not have to be a chore. In fact, when you try something new it can become a fun new hobby. If you want to get more exercise in but don't enjoy the treadmill, try signing up for a yoga class, joining a bowling league, or dropping in on a dance class.

Reading

Reading is the perfect way to escape daily life and find enjoyment and fun while never even leaving home. What's great about reading is that even though it will feel like relaxing, it will keep your mind active and stimulated. I have tons of books in my home and I am always reading a book, sometimes fiction, sometimes non-fiction. You can also read to the person you are taking care of and both of you can enjoy a good novel at the same time.

Whatever hobby you choose, remember to relax and enjoy the moment.

Chapter 20
LAUGH A LOT

I would be negligent if I didn't tell you to keep your sense of humor. Sometimes we have to laugh to keep from crying! One of the most therapeutic ways of surviving the stresses and trials of life is by having a sense of humor. Humor has a way of calming the soul and releasing the pressure of worry, guilt, shame, or regret. A sense of humor gives an optimistic view in looking at my present situation and my future. I wasn't always in a space where I could laugh, but I have come to see life through better lenses and a lot of that has to do with humor. I could not have survived being a special needs parent without laughter. My daughter is responsible for a lot of those laughs and I encourage you to not lose your sense of humor during your caregiving journey. "Pain is inevitable, misery is optional."

Chapter 21
TAKE CARE OF YOUR SPIRITUALITY

Spirituality is a way we find meaning and inner peace in life. Some people find spirituality in religion. Other people find spirituality through art, nature, or their values. No matter your beliefs, your spiritual health is important, so don't take it lightly.

What Do You Need to Know?

It's a fact that caregivers often sacrifice their own well-being to provide care for others. This sacrifice can disrupt your beliefs and cause spiritual distress. Symptoms of spiritual distress include:

- Loss of purpose or meaning
- Questioning your faith, values, and beliefs
- Feeling abandoned or punished by God
- Feeling worthless, hopeless, and alone in the world
- Withdrawal from family and friends

Why is spirituality important to your health?

There seems to be a connection between the mind, body, and spirit. When you have spiritual distress, your entire being is affected. While physical health is easy to measure, spiritual health is not. Being healthy spiritually means showing love to yourself and others. You have a sense of inner peace and contentment. You value life and are thankful for what you have. Being spiritually healthy can help you cope with the stress of being a caregiver.

What to Discuss with Healthcare Team

Talk to your healthcare provider if you are feeling spiritual distress. Your provider can refer you to a local clergyman or spiritual advisor. If you attend a house of worship, speak to your pastor or priest. Ask your healthcare provider about support groups in your area.

Helpful Tips

Think about what nourishes your spirit and makes you feel at peace. Set aside time each day to practice these things. This may include:

- Practicing prayer or meditation. Some people find prayer or meditation to be helpful. Benefits include lower stress and better overall health.
- Volunteering in the community. Helping others can put your problems into perspective. It can also provide you with a sense of purpose and pride.

- Read the Bible or other inspirational books. Some people find comfort in God's word. Reading about other's triumphs over adversity can inspire you.
- Attend a house of worship. Some people find a sense of community when surrounded by others who share their beliefs.
- Go on a nature walk. Connecting with nature can bring spiritual peace.
- Keep a journal to express your thoughts and feelings. Writing down your problems can help you sort them out.

Remember

- Strengthening your spiritual side can help you cope with the stress of caregiving.
- There seems to be a connection between the mind, body, and spirit. When you have spiritual distress, other areas of your body and mind are affected.
- Think about what nourishes your spirit and makes you feel at peace. Set aside time every day to practice these things.

Chapter 22
GRATITUDE

If you are reading this book and you are a caregiver, know that the work you do as a caregiver is far from easy. It requires not just physical energy but mental discipline and emotional stamina. It requires long days and even longer nights and not just sometimes, but day after day. Much is asked of you and much is needed from you. Sometimes it may seem that your work is never done. Sometimes it may seem that you never get enough sleep. Sometimes it may seem that you are all alone.

It may feel as if the responsibilities are too much to bear and that no one cares. Additionally, you may not hear many words of appreciation or see many signs of support. If any of this resonates with you, know this: you are doing important work even if the recognition is overlooked and even if gratitude is in short supply. You are making a difference in the life of someone else and that difference runs deeper than you can ever know .

Chapter 23
Volunteering

Everyone is busy. Busy happens whether you are currently a caregiver or not. I do not have time to volunteer, I make time to volunteer. The benefits of volunteering are enormous to you, your family, and your community. Last year I began a yearlong commitment as a Civic Leader with Hands on Atlanta. I was assigned to a non-profit named InCommunity (formally enAble Ga). Among other services, InCommunity provides housing to developmentally disabled adults. I will admit they were not my first choice, they were not even my second choice, they were my third. I was reluctant to become their Civic Leader because I thought it would be too emotional an assignment because I have a daughter with a developmental disability. My fears were unwarranted. As the Civic Leader for InCommunity, my preconceived notion of what a home for the developmentally disabled would look like has been replaced with the truth of how well these homes are operated and how much pride the residents have in a place they call home. Volunteering can be truly rewarding. My daughter receives respite services from this organization and some of the Saturdays that I am serving them, there is someone serving her and making sure she is safe and having a good time with her peer group. In addition to servings as a Civic Leader, I also serve as a volunteer Advocate Ambassador for Autism Speaks where I advocate for policies and programs in support of individuals and families with autism. Autism Speaks has given me the opportunity to talk with Congressmen and Senators and have a better appreciation for the work that goes into passing laws that directly affect my family. I had the opportunity to travel to Washington D. C. for Autism Speaks Hill Day which was a truly exciting experience. Volunteering has rewards and benefits. Find your right match and you can reduce stress, find friends, reach out to the community, learn new skills, and even advance your career. Giving to others can also help protect your mental and physical health. As you can see from my experiences volunteering offers vital help to people in need, it can give you a sense of purpose when you connect with a worthwhile cause and the benefits can be even greater for you, the volunteer. While it's true that the more you volunteer, the more benefits you'll experience, volunteering doesn't have to involve a long-term commitment or take a huge amount of time out of your busy day. Giving in even simple ways can help others. Whatever city you call home you can Google volunteer opportunities and find a match, close to home. Give it a try.

Chapter 24
PAPERWORK

The process to obtain disability benefits for my daughter has always been frustrating. I have stacks and stacks of paperwork accumulated over the years from applying for benefits. I wish there was a universal form to fill out to save parents/caregivers from the paperwork nightmare. Start this process on a day when you have time to concentrate because it's a lot of work. Always KEEP COPIES of anything you submit and make notes on your copies of the date submitted, and if you spoke on the telephone with anyone, write down the whole name, date, and time and a short synopsis of what was said. This will save you from becoming fed up with the nightmare of applying for benefits.

Chapter 25
9 to 5

There was a time when I hated working the night shift, but after I became a mother I felt night shift was a blessing. I am grateful I had a job with the options to work any hours I chose to. It is unfortunate that many people have had to quit their jobs or retire early in order to serve as a family caregiver. Many more struggle to juggle caregiving and their career.

Working family caregivers often manage to stay at work by arranging for a flexible schedule, cutting back their hours, switching to a different type of job, or arranging to work from home. If you are a caregiver and work full-time here are a few suggestions.

Human Resources

- Ask your HR rep about company policies and programs to support caregivers. Many companies have a plan in place to help employees find community services, counseling, respite care, legal and financial assistance, and caregiver support groups. Others offer caregiving leave or flexible work arrangements.

- Some employers may not have a policy for employees who are also caregivers, but they may be open to the idea. If yours is, tell them what would help you and colleagues in the same situation. Ask if they'd consider starting a trial program.

- Employee assistance or your loved one's insurance carrier might cover visits with a therapist specializing in caretaking or family issues. Sometimes one small thing can be a big help.

- Be prepared: Even within the same company, different managers may be more or less supportive.

Talk to Your Manager

If you work for a small company with no HR department, make an appointment with your boss. Be upfront about your caregiving responsibilities from the start. Most bosses value good employees and will work to keep them.

- Don't go in with the idea that there is a single answer.

- Present solutions that won't cost the company money or time.

- Flextime and telecommuting are accepted practices in many offices.

- Employers may be more likely to agree if you suggest a trial period that could be continued if successful.

- Be ready to compromise. A flexible schedule might not be possible, but your company may be willing to change your schedule, let you work from home one day a week, or pay for respite care when you travel for work.

- If your supervisor lets you work from home, make sure you are always accessible by phone and email. Respond quickly.

- Attend meetings from home by conference call or Skype. If Skyping, find a quiet room where you won't be interrupted and dress as you would at the office.

Family and Medical Leave Act (FMLA)

Under the Family and Medical Leave Act, eligible workers are entitled to unpaid leave for up to 12 weeks per year without losing job security or health benefits, to care for a spouse, child, or parent who has a serious health condition.

- Companies that employ fewer than 50 people are exempt from FMLA.

- To qualify, you must have worked for the company for at least 1,250 hours in the last 12 months. Check with your HR department to see if you qualify. The company is required by law to tell you your rights under FMLA and, if you qualify, offer you leave. Employers may not threaten you or make your work life difficult because you requested a leave.

• You may take the 12 weeks of leave all at once or in pieces — for example, three days twice a month when a parent is receiving chemotherapy. When your leave is up, you must return to work to protect your job.

• Under the Americans With Disabilities Act (ADA), employees taking time off to care for a disabled parent or spouse are entitled to the same treatment as coworkers who take time off to care for disabled children.

• The ADA also gives you protection if you lose your job or are harassed.

• Some states have laws similar to, but not identical, to the federal FMLA. They may provide different benefits.

Chapter 26
IS IT TOO MUCH?

One of my daughter's doctors once told me that I should prepare myself for the day when I would have to place her in a facility. I was offended. I knew that I would never consider placing her in an assisted living facility; it was out of the question. Since that day there have been a couple of other people who have asked me if maybe that would be best. I do not judge parents or families who choose to go that route; however, that is not the route for me. I have let my son (who is my daughter's co-legal guardian) know that it would be fine with me if he decides (when I pass away) to place Tylar in an assisted living facility. It's a hard decision. I am trying to make it easier by planning ahead and getting all of her paperwork and waivers in place should he decide to do so. He has watched and helped me take care of his sister his entire life, so he knows what a huge undertaking it would be. If you've been a caregiver for a long time, you know just how hard it can be. Perhaps, at first, you were more than willing to take on the job because you knew what it meant to your loved one. Perhaps you are caregiving for your own child and, like me, it is the natural thing to do. Maybe you managed the first few weeks or months or even years with ease, running from work to errands to taking care of your other children, your loved one — and back again. You played phone tag with doctors, scheduled treatments, and even played chauffeur. The lack of free time you had to yourself maybe didn't seem like such a big deal in comparison to the job of being a good parent, son, or daughter.

But over time, the pressures of caregiving can weigh anyone down. Feeling constantly stressed out and exhausted, it's easy to stop going to your own doctor's appointments, which can take a toll on your own health. Since you've been taking care of another person, maybe your social life has become non-existent, or you've seen your work attendance decline. If these scenarios about caregiver stress sound all too familiar to you, you may need to consider taking a break from being a caregiver. This is not an easy choice to make and can be even more difficult if it's your child. Outside help can be of tremendous value to a family caregiver; these are professionals who have previous related experience with any number of health conditions. They know what to do, when to do it, and how to do it. Equally important, involving a healthcare professional in your loved one's care will free up your own time to enjoy some much-needed respite.

The questions are not so much when to reach out for additional help (this will vary dramatically depending on the situation and one's readiness to make that decision), but instead, how do you find, hire, and involve these workers with your loved one? This is a serious matter. You need to find someone who is experienced, qualified, responsible, trustworthy, and conscientious. Personally, my best resource is to ask other parents how they find professionals to work with their sons and daughters. There are several agencies who vet respite workers and I only need to do the in-person interview. If you are a caregiver for an aging parent, you can reach out to senior agencies for resources and recommendations.

Now is not the time to be shy about asking questions. After all, you are representing your loved one's best interests. Ask your friends, family members, church members, and loved one's doctors for recommendations. When hiring a private caregiver, make sure they are a good fit for your child or parent. You can start out slowly by having them work one or two days a week in the beginning and increase the days after they are comfortable with the job. Hire someone who has warmth, compassion, empathy, and an interest other than just collecting a check. It takes time to become comfortable with the idea of receiving help. And you will come to appreciate it.

Remember to also accommodate your care worker as much as possible. He or she will be spending a great deal of time with your loved one. Be sure to outline your expectations fully. For example, do you need laundry done or meals cooked? If so, make that clear up front. If he or she is coming into your loved one's home, leave notes as to where to find the cleaning supplies, the can opener, the extra towels, and so on. Provide your phone number(s) in case of emergency. And if your caregiver is taking your loved one outside of the home/care facility, also supply a small cash float for any incurred expenses (you can ask for receipts in exchange).

As a final word, please don't hesitate to ask for caregiving help when and where needed. Don't attempt to force family members to be caregivers when their plate is already full and don't guilt them into it. Have a conversation and be honest about how you feel. When bringing in the right person (or the right people), both you and your loved one will benefit. When you signed on to be a caregiver, it wasn't supposed to take over your life. Indeed, too much caregiver stress can spell disaster — for both you and your loved one. It's much more beneficial to both of you, as well as your family, if you know your limits.

Remember that caregiving isn't for everyone. Take a minute to recognize how strong you are to have made it this far. I can honestly tell you that I have come a long, long, long way on the caregiving road and have further roads to travel, but I'm here and I wake up and give it my best every day.

Chapter 27
THINK POSITIVE, KEEP HOPE ALIVE

I give a lot of thought to the importance of having hope, dreams, gratitude, and purpose in my life and I encourage you to do the same. I wake up every day grateful with a sense of purpose, dreams I want to work toward, and hope that I will achieve them. It is my belief that there is not a caregiver alive that doesn't have a desire for a purposeful life. Just because you are a caregiver is not a good reason to abandon the goals, dreams, purpose, and ideas you have for your life. These things are a part of life and human nature. We all have the inbred desire for a good life. Hope is vital to the life of every person, whether you are giving care or receiving care.

The definition of hope is the feeling of wanting something to happen and thinking that it could happen. While hope is vital, it is also important to have positive thoughts. You have probably had someone tell you to "look on the bright side" or to "see the cup as half full." Chances are good that the people who make these comments are positive thinkers. Researchers are finding more and more evidence pointing to the many benefits of optimism and positive thinking.

Such findings suggest that not only are positive thinkers healthier and less stressed, they also have greater overall well-being.

As adults, we realize that life happens and there are bound to be some disappointments and setbacks are inherent to almost every worthwhile human activity, and a number of studies show that optimists are in general both psychologically and physiologically healthier.

Even if positive thinking does not come naturally to you, there are plenty of great reasons to start cultivating affirmative thoughts and minimizing negative self-talk.

Positive Thinkers Cope Better with Stress

When faced with stressful situations, positive thinkers cope more effectively than pessimists. In one study, researchers found that when optimists encounter a disappointment (such as not getting a job or promotion), they are more likely to focus on things they can do to resolve the situation.

Rather than dwelling on their frustrations or things that they cannot change, they will devise a plan of action and ask others for assistance and advice. Pessimists, on the other hand, simply assume that the situation is out of their control and there is nothing they can do to change it.

Optimism Can Improve Your Immunity

In recent years, researchers have found that your mind can have a powerful effect on your body. Immunity is one area where your thoughts and attitudes can have a particularly powerful influence. In one study, researchers found that activation in brain areas associated with negative emotions led to a weaker immune response to a flu vaccine.

Researchers have found that people who were optimistic about a specific and important part of their lives, such as how well they were doing in school, exhibited a stronger immune response than those who had a more negative view of the situation. Always see your cup as half full if not full.

Positive Thinking Is Good for Your Health

Not only can positive thinking impact your ability to cope with stress and your immunity, it also has an impact on your overall well-being. The Mayo Clinic reports a number of health benefits associated with optimism, including a reduced risk of death from cardiovascular problems, less depression, and an increased lifespan. Because heart disease runs in my family this is of special attention for me.

While researchers are not entirely clear on why positive thinking benefits health, some suggest that positive people might lead healthier lifestyles. By coping better with stress and avoiding unhealthy behaviors, they are able to improve their health and well-being.

It Can Make You More Resilient

Resilience refers to our ability to cope with problems. Resilient people are able to face a crisis or trauma with strength and resolve. Rather than falling apart in the face of such stress, they have the ability to carry on and eventually overcome such adversity. It may come as no surprise to learn that positive thinking can play a major role in resilience.

When dealing with a challenge, optimists typically look at what they can do to fix the problem. Instead of giving up hope, they marshal their resources and are willing to ask others for help.

Researchers have also found that in the wake of a crisis, such as a terrorist attack or natural disaster, positive thoughts and emotions encourage thriving and provide a sort of buffer against depression among resilient people. Fortunately, experts also believe that such positivism and resilience can be cultivated. By nurturing positive emotions, even in the face of terrible events, people can reap both short-term and long-term rewards, including managing stress levels, lessening depression, and building coping skills that will serve them well in the future.

Chapter 28
EXPRESS YOURSELF

It is common to spend so much of your time caring for others that you end up ignoring, holding back, or failing to recognize your own feelings about the situation. Continuously ignoring your own feelings can be very dangerous. Feelings can build up until you become so stressed that you can no longer handle the situation. I frequently have feelings of fear. Having the diagnosis of autism and not knowing my daughter's future prospects makes me fearful. What is going to happen to her as she grows older? What is going to happen to her when I am gone? Then other questions arise: Will she ever live on her own? Will she ever have friends? Fear can immobilize you if you let it. Fear of the future only depletes the energy of the present so try to take one step, one day at a time. I also have feelings of loneliness, confusion, disappointment, powerlessness, and sometimes I just want to lay in bed and cry. It's okay to have these feelings, and it is extremely important for you to identify and address the feelings that you are having. Here are some specific, appropriate ways to express and cope with your emotions.

Tips for expressing your feelings:

Identify what it is that you are feeling and allow yourself to accept the emotions as a natural response to caregiving.
Do not bottle up your feelings.
Share what you are feeling with the patient if you feel it's appropriate.
Call a close friend or family member with whom you can discuss your feelings. I reach out to parents in autism groups and they can relate to what I'm feeling.
Write down your thoughts and feelings in a private journal.
Join a local support group for caregivers or families of ill patients.
Get a referral from your doctor and speak to a professional therapist who can help you understand and deal with your emotions. If you are employed, your employer may also provide outside resources that are available at low or no cost.
Speak to a chaplain, priest, rabbi, minister, or another religious figure if you trust them.

Chapter 29
GOLDEN YEARS

Are you caring for mom or dad? You are not alone. 65% of seniors who need long-term care rely exclusively on family and friends. 50% of seniors who have no family to care for them are in nursing homes. Sometimes family members feel as though they do not have a choice when it comes to taking care of their aging parents. On average a caregiver will spend no less than 24 hours providing care despite the fact that most have full-time jobs. The facts are that caregivers who experience extreme stress age prematurely, shaving as much as 10 years off their lives, and they are more likely to experience anxiety, depression, and chronic disease than non-caregivers. Most family caregivers are ill-prepared for their role and provide care with little or zero support. My sister volunteered to take care of my mother and, like most older caregivers, she has experienced issues such as stress and poor health herself. Caregiving is hard work and I am a big proponent of asking for help. Hiring helpers does not mean you don't love your parents; it means you love your parents yet recognize that you are only human and can only do so much. If you have a plan B in place, you will not have to scramble around and panic if your plan A fails. If you are taking care of your elderly parents, take the time to discuss what will happen if you happen to become ill and are unable to provide adequate care. This way you can avoid having chaos further complicate a delicate situation.

Chapter 30
YOU ARE NOT ALONE

The feeling of isolation during the time of giving your all to care for others is almost universal among caregivers. I hope the words, advice, and recommendations in this book help you handle feelings of separateness and isolation and help you understand the importance of taking care of YOU. It helps to know that these feelings have been experienced by many, many others, that understanding and constructive help are available to you and whoever you are caring for, and that you are not alone. As we work tirelessly to help those in need, we wonder if anyone out there knows what we do as caregivers and how hard it can be. But we are not alone. There are a lot more of us out there than you think. And at one point, we will all become caregivers or need a caregiver.

Today, there are more than 50 million caregivers in the United States and millions more worldwide. That's 35 percent of the adult population. Tomorrow, there will be even more. What ties us together is that we're all in it to help someone. We're a big, caring family that is growing by the day.

In my case, I learned how to become a caregiver when my daughter was diagnosed with autism. Of course, becoming a caregiver was not what I wanted, but I had to take care of my daughter. One in 59 children has autism and most of them are male. I feel very special having a daughter. I was already a mom to a son and I became a mom again and a caregiver to a beautiful girl who I nurture, teach and guide each day. As I write this, my daughter is 25 years old. She has been through more than a lot of ladies her age. She will never live on her own, never marry, never become a mother. Those are the thoughts I have had to reconcile myself with. I will be a caregiver until I can no longer physically care for her and I hope that it's the rest of my life. My daughter's autism became my education to caregiving, and to life, really. I learned the hard way. I'm still learning.

Now, I don't have all the answers to be a caregiver, but I can provide some guidance as to what can make your experience and the experience of others a lot more positive and healing. There can be anger, sadness, guilt, remorse. There is a physical strain, emotional stress, and financial hardship. But, remember, you're there to help someone. You are their guide, their hand to hold, the one with answers in a world that can be filled with questions and worry.

Above all, remember there are many caregivers out there alongside you, working hard to ensure the best for their loved one or care recipient. You're not alone, and with the words in this book, you can be confident you're giving your best care for them as well as for yourself.

Chapter 31
RESENTMENT

Resentment is such a touchy subject. Every person has their own point of view and life experience, so before you fall into the trap of resentment, at the very least try to walk in the other person's shoes. Resentment takes many forms. If you are a caregiver taking care of your aging parent, you may have experienced sibling resentment as a caregiver or seen your sibling relationships deteriorate due to disagreements about care. Arguments threaten to flare up over issues like sharing responsibility for care, methods of care, living arrangements, etc. These are touchy topics at best but, as I said before, everyone has their own point of view and life experiences.

Sharing care responsibilities

One of the most common reasons for siblings fighting over elderly parents is who takes responsibility for the care of Mom or Dad. Even if all siblings want to help look after their parents, not all have the time and energy to do this. The challenge here is that everyone has different commitments and different priorities. Someone who has more flexible work hours, or fewer childcare commitments, isn't necessarily able to devote more time to caregiving or can drop everything to help out on a regular basis.

This situation may be compounded by differences in locations. Children who live further away find it much more difficult to regularly visit and contribute to the caregiving effort. They may want to help but can't or may not even realize they aren't doing their fair share. The sibling who does take on more might assume that the others have just decided this arrangement makes more sense when they never even had that thought.

Solution: It is difficult to decide how to divide who does what. A parent's slow decline may mean you end up in roles without meaning to, and responsibilities might become unevenly shared. Or, the role may just be assumed out of necessity. It can be a struggle to decide who should do what and come to an agreement where it feels like everyone is pulling their weight. Communication is the only way around this. Avoid choosing who will be the caregiver by proxy. If you can, talk about the prospect of caring for your elderly parents before it becomes an urgent matter. If you've already fallen into established roles, call a family meeting to discuss how you can find an arrangement that suits everyone better. If you volunteered to be the caregiver and it has become too big a job for you, have a family meeting with your siblings and discuss how to take some of the pressure off of you and come up with an agreed-upon plan. Allow your siblings to have responsibilities that they feel comfortable doing and everyone gains. Your brother may be a good advocate and the perfect person to take Mom/Dad to doctor appointments. Your sister may be a good cook and able to plan meals. Finally, if you have volunteered to be a caregiver for your parents, do not alienate your siblings out of resentment for not doing what you assume they should be doing. Communicate.

Chapter 32
MI CASA SU CASA

Other feuds may arise over where and who your parents will live with. In my case, my sister moved in with my parents when she retired. They were not immobile, but they were aging, on medication, and going to doctor appointments regularly. My father became ill and eventually passed away. When my mother fell and broke her hip a few years ago my sister was already there to help her get back on her feet, which she never did. Over the years I have warned my sister about caregiver burnout, and I've even volunteered for my mother to come live with me. My mother wants to stay in her own home and I understand how she feels, but what happens when my sister becomes ill? It's a hard conversation to have when you are the daughter/sister/caregiver trying to do what you think is best for everyone only to be met with pushback. Once again, communication is key. I've stated how I feel and why I think it's best, but ultimately my mother wants to stay in her home, so I have suggested we hire part-time help. Unfortunately, that suggestion has also been met with pushback, but at least I tried. Now is not the time to argue, but to instead leave the lines of communication open. Circumstances may change. Your parent may be in their home this year and move in with you or one of your siblings later. My mother knows she always has a home with me. I'm keeping my door open and I suggest you do the same.

Chapter 33
I'M THE BOSS, NO I'M THE BOSS

No one person must oversee everything. Resentment starts to brew when one sibling believes it's their given right to rule over everyone and everything. Bossy controlling behavior brings out the worst in everyone. Grown-up siblings will not be content to continue the same hierarchies as they did as children, and it can be equally hard for older siblings to realize they are not "king of the castle" and younger siblings are not their "subjects" to rule over. Nothing is more stressful for a parent who must become a mediator because one sibling wants to be king. Siblings love their parents and want what is best for them, and parents love all of you equally. Now is not the time for arguing. Put your egos aside and concentrate on what is best for your mother and father. You may have to bite your tongue for your sake and theirs. Remember, you can't control other people but you can control yourself. If you can't come to a resolution, give it a couple of days of rest and try talking about it later. If you find yourself not making any progress toward a resolution, perhaps asking your parents' doctor for advice as to what is best would be a good step. Do not let your relationship with your sibling degrade to the point that you are no longer speaking to each other. Life is too short.

Chapter 34
COIN CONTRIBUTION

Who pays for what can lead to one of the most explosive aspects of caregiving that can generate sibling resentment.

Your elderly parents may be on a limited income and not be able to afford the rising cost of care. Assisted living communities, mortgages, nursing homes, medication, etc. all cost money, and siblings don't always have it.

Whether children should contribute towards care cost if their parents cannot afford it is a difficult matter. More controversially, how much should they pay? Should they forgo things they need or want to help aging parents?

This can be a very touchy subject if siblings aren't in similar financial situations. Should a high earner contribute more? And what if they have higher living costs, for example, if they are supporting a larger family? Further, just because someone appears financially comfortable, that doesn't necessarily mean they have the cash to spare.

Perceptions and reality don't always match when it comes to money, and different people have very different priorities about spending. It's also difficult to decide how much financial contribution can or should count as a substitute for in-person assistance. Also, if one sibling is seen as having the time to look after their parent, others may be reluctant to pay for a professional caregiver — even though they aren't able to do the job themselves. It's highly likely that everyone has a different view of what is "fair."

Solution: Talking about money with your siblings can be one of the most difficult things to do. Everyone can have different ideas about what they can or should afford, but you can feel like they are being cheap or stingy.

Money is a very personal matter, and you don't always know what's going on with your siblings behind the scenes. You also can't force anyone to part with their money if they don't want to give it. It might help if you come up with a budget for the care plan you have in mind to make it very tangible how much is needed and how it will be spent. If your sibling understands, they may be more inclined to contribute. Ask what they think they can give and accept their answer. Remember, it's not your place to make demands over their money.

Chapter 35
THIS NOT THAT

Caregiving siblings may fight and have conflicting opinions about what is best for their parents, especially if they have different caregiving styles.

These struggles can be difficult and bitter, especially if the one with daily caring responsibilities feels criticized by siblings who are not present day to day. It's easy to mistake suggestions or comments as criticism when you are playing such a tough and emotionally demanding role. I have made the mistake of making comments that were said out of concern, but which were taken out of context. To those caregivers who are present every day, remember that siblings love and want the best for their parents, the same as you do. When your parents' time is up it's not just the primary caregiver that grieves; it's all the siblings. Communicate directly and regularly with your siblings so you each have a chance to have an active role in your parents' last days. Share care plans and perhaps a care diary so everyone feels involved. Listen to suggestions from everyone and let go of the need to be right. Consider that everyone is feeling emotional and try not to take anything personally. Grudges will not help anyone, least of all the person holding them.

In a perfect world, we'd all work together peacefully to give our parents the best end of life in return for the love and support they gave us. It rarely works out that way, but that doesn't mean we shouldn't try.

If you are arguing with your siblings or feeling upset or resentful about care matters, you are not alone. It's normal. You don't need to feel guilty for being emotional at this tough time. Communication is key. It doesn't take much to have a conversation.

Remember, you're not doing this for yourself, you're doing it for your parents. Focus on what is best for them. Try to stay calm and reasoned. And, most importantly of all, try to stay friends with your brothers and sisters; you know that's what your parents would want.

Chapter 36
HAVE A PLAN B

Life is full of surprises and it's been said life is nothing but change. Life will throw you curveballs and sometimes good things happen, and sometimes bad things happen. As a caregiver, it's almost inevitable that life will throw you a surprise from time to time. Sometimes the surprises are pleasant. Sometimes the surprises will undermine your primary Plan. Because we don't have a magic ball to see into the future, we need to have a Plan B. Sadly, most caregivers do not have a Plan B. Considering what would happen in a crisis is too painful to consider a backup plan.

Consider this: What would happen if you collapse and die and the person you are caring for is unable to call for help? What if you become ill and need emergency surgery followed by a stay in the hospital and the person you are caring for is unable to walk or prepare their own meal?

If you are a caregiver without a Plan B, you are doing the person you are caring for a great disservice. Plan for the worst and pray for the best. Get out of your feelings and create a workable Plan B for yourself, as well as for the person needing care because you cannot foresee when a crisis will come. It's impossible to prepare for every emergency or crisis, but give some serious thought to what may happen if you become incapacitated. Here are some Plan B considerations:

1.   Have a family plan in place in the event you become ill. List all medications your loved one takes, doctor names, monthly obligations. Other family members should not be in the dark and starting from scratch simply because you don't have a backup plan.
2.   Check with assisted living communities that offer respite or short-term stays. Inquire as to the process of having your loved one on a list, and fill out the paperwork just in case an emergency happens.
3.   Ask someone near you to volunteer to be an emergency care provider in the event you become ill and unable to provide care. Consider purchasing a medical alert device. What happens if you leave the house and have a car accident? What happens if the house catches fire while you run to the store and your loved one is incapacitated in the bed?

It doesn't hurt anyone to have a Plan B, but not having a backup plan has the potential to hurt everyone.

Chapter 37
KEEP DREAMING

Before you put on those rose-colored glasses, it is important to note that positive thinking is not about taking a "Pollyanna" approach to life. In fact, researchers have found that in some instances, optimism might not serve you well. For example, people who are excessively optimistic might overestimate their own abilities and take on more than they can handle, ultimately leading to more stress and anxiety.

Instead of ignoring reality in favor of the silver lining, psychologists suggest that positive thinking should center on such things as a belief in your abilities, a positive approach to challenges, and trying to make the most of the bad situations. Bad things will happen. Sometimes you will be disappointed or hurt by the actions of others. This does not mean that the world is out to get you or that all people will let you down. Instead, positive thinkers will look at the situation realistically, search for ways that they can improve the situation, and try to learn from their experiences.

Every human being dreams, and the dreams differ greatly from person to person, some being small while others are unrealistically large. Whatever the case is, it gives us something to look forward to; for example, dreaming about becoming a rich executive helps us to focus on doing well at school to achieve this goal, so without these dreams, our lives would be empty and pointless.

Dreams are what make us what we are. Everyone has a different dream and these dreams are what influence our whole lives. Without hope, a person has no motivation. There would be no point in going to school or getting a job since no one would hope to have a career or family. Hope is what motivates us and keeps us going through the hard times. We dream of something better than we presently have, and it is a dream of having a successful job and a family that motivate us to succeed in achieving our goals.

"All men who have achieved great things have been great dreamers," said Orison Swett Marden. Any person that has achieved something great had a dream first. A famous and obvious example is Martin Luther King, Jr., who said, "I have a dream!" It was that dream that changed the way people thought and made them stop and think. If he had not dreamed, he never would have stood up for what he believed in and never would have aimed to change things. This is exactly why we need dreams — to have hope and to aim to change our present situation for the better.

Dreams change as we get older and some are less important than others but however trivial or small the dreams are, they are still important since they bring some sense into our lives, giving it some sort of purpose. Without these dreams, our lives would be empty.

Chapter 38
REWARDS

"A gift opens the way and ushers the giver into the presence of the great." — Proverbs 18:16

For every action, the universe provides a reaction so, while caregiving comes with its challenges, it also provides great rewards. While most of this book covers the challenges you can face as a caregiver and the importance of taking care of yourself while caregiving, there are many rewards for your work and the care that you give.

Making a difference in a life.

There is a big reward for being able to be present, connecting, and caring for someone who cannot fully care for themselves. When I help my daughter with bathing it not only makes her feel good, but she is learning how to perform this task on her own. As caregivers, we are needed and depended on more than we realize. The opportunity to strengthen bonds and create memories is invaluable. Caregiving is a great opportunity to bring the family together for a common cause. I have met new friends during my caregiver journey and you can do the same by connecting with other like-minded caregivers, be it family caregivers or professional caregivers.

Knowledge

Knowledge is a reward to which we give little credit. If you think back to when your caregiving journey began and where you are now, you probably have a wealth of knowledge to pass along to those beginning their journey. You may not have taken the time or not have the time yet to sit down and think about all that you have learned. I suggest you start a journal if you haven't already. Write down your daily thoughts and record what you have learned and what your takeaways are. You can be a tremendous resource to others. Your knowledge can be used to begin a new career or start a business. You are setting an example and leading future generations.

Giving back

Giving back is the greatest reward. In between the hectic schedules, doctor appointments, and lack of sleep, there is still that sense of satisfaction at the end of the day. You have kept someone safe, fed, and comfortable. You are a hero.

Chapter 39
TAKE CARE, YOU MATTER

In my experience, caring for a child who has autism is the ultimate labor of love. Your child always needs you and you need to be there for your child. Yet, despite your best intentions, there are recurring moments in every parent/caregiver's life when this effort becomes too overwhelming. The non-stop care, support, and guidance can chip away at even the most strong-willed parents. Even the strongest parent/caregiver needs an occasional break. It took me years to realize that "I matter" and, likewise, your emotional, mental, and physical health matter. Your feelings matter. Your dreams and life passions matter.

We become so engulfed in providing care for others that we sometimes get lost. We become secondary. All of your days will not be perfect, but all anyone can do is their best. You are not alone. You'll be amazed at how many people are experiencing similar life situations and the strength and support that results from simply reaching out. You matter, so remember that it is not selfish to focus on your own needs and desires when you are a caregiver — it's an important part of the job. You are responsible for your own self-care. Focus on the chapters in this book and practice self-care.

Chapter 40
TAKE CARE TIMESAVERS FOR CAREGIVERS

1 Plan tomorrow the night before. I'm a big advocate of writing down my goals and plans on paper so I can see what I need to do the next day. Planning keeps me on track. I know what time I need to get my day started to accomplish my goals for the day.

2 Plan all meals and cook enough to have leftovers. I love leftovers, so I cook with the intent of having leftovers for the days ahead. Sometimes I freeze meals to save time for the days ahead.

3 Shop online when possible. I love Amazon and they sell everything. I have Amazon Prime and it pays for itself with the money I save on shipping. This saves me trips to the store, and I don't always desire to take my daughter to the store with me because of her sometimes-upsetting behavior. I can shop online and walk out my door and pick up my box. I haven't tried Instacart yet, but I hear it is convenient as well, and there are other places where you

can order your entire meal and they will deliver all the ingredients you need to cook the meal.

4 Record the shows you want to watch and save them for a convenient time to watch. TV and the internet are time suckers and before you know it you have wasted your day either watching TV or mindlessly surfing the internet.

5 Keep a folder of important paperwork in a backpack. It should have power of attorney, a copy of the health care proxy, a copy of the advance directive, and a list of medications. If you have to go to the hospital with an emergency, you will have all the needed information in one place. Simply grab the backpack on the way out the door so there's no scrambling around for information in the middle of an emergency. Your backpack should also have a small blanket or sweater (waiting rooms are always cold). Keep some toiletries, a paperback book, and a phone charger, and snacks or coins for the snack machine as well.

6 Investigate and participate in your local caregiving community. An adult day care program is good for socialization and structure and has activities designed to maintain or strengthen skills. It may help you to talk to others who are facing the same issues. You also may be able to find people with whom you can have a mutual backup agreement or share a part-time caregiver.

7 Minimize the time you take away from your job. Schedule your loved one's doctor and therapy appointments early in the morning or at the end of the day.

8 Manage your time efficiently. Set priorities. Tackle the most important items first. When you are stretched between two obligations, it's easy to forget something. Keep focused by using two to-do lists — one for caregiving

and one for work. Put obligations for both caregiving and work on a single calendar. Delegate at work and at home.

Remember that caregiving isn't for everyone. Take a minute to recognize how strong you are to have made it this far. I can honestly tell you that I have come a long, long, long way on the caregiving road and have further roads to travel but I'm here and I wake up and give it my best every day. So, if no one pats you on the back today, give yourself a pat on the back and say job well done.

You Matter

Living a promise,

working day and night.

Commitments you make

to family, friends, work and all.

No time to smell roses or watch the sunset.

Feelings overwhelmed, your dreams unfulfilled.

Intimacy shattered and no one to talk to,

friendships faded and love on the rocks.

Deliver yourself from fear and frustration.

Deliver your mind from thoughts of worry.

Let the tears roll free, to let out all the sadness.

Give others a chance to share in the care,

a chance to give back before it's too late.

Reach out to the world,

refresh your perspective.

Dare caring for you, both your body and soul.

Take care of yourself and be who you are,

you have dreams to fulfill while able and strong.

Embrace your life, the gift you were given,

take care of you too, life is too short know that you matter.

Renewed, you can blossom,

freed up from the burden of guilt and despair.

Reborn, love can flourish,

and your care can become a blessing to share.

Made in the USA
Columbia, SC
13 June 2018